ILLUMINATED
SCRIPTURE JOURNAL

ENGLISH STANDARD VERSION

ROMANS

CROSSWAY

WHEATON, ILLINOIS — ESV.ORG

PREFACE

The Bible

The words of the Bible are the very words of God our Creator speaking to us. They are completely truthful;[1] they are pure;[2] they are powerful;[3] and they are wise and righteous.[4] We should read these words with reverence and awe,[5] and with joy and delight.[6] Through these words God gives us eternal life,[7] and daily nourishes our spiritual lives.[8]

The ESV Translation

The English Standard Version® (ESV®) stands in the classic stream of English Bible translations that goes back nearly five centuries. In this stream, accurate faithfulness to the original text is combined with simplicity, beauty, and dignity of expression. Our goal has been to carry forward this legacy for this generation and generations to come.

The ESV is an "essentially literal" translation that seeks as far as possible to reproduce the meaning and structure of the original text and the personal style of each Bible writer. We have sought to be "as literal as possible" while maintaining clear expression and literary excellence. Therefore the ESV is well suited for both personal reading and church ministry, for devotional reflection and serious study, and for Scripture memorization.

---

[1] Ps. 119:160; Prov. 30:5; Titus 1:2; Heb. 6:18 [2] Ps. 12:6 [3] Jer. 23:29; Heb. 4:12; 1 Pet. 1:23
[4] Ps. 19:7–11 [5] Deut. 28:58; Ps. 119:74; Isa. 66:2 [6] Ps. 19:7–11; 119:14, 97, 103; Jer. 15:16
[7] John 6:68; 1 Pet. 1:23 [8] Deut. 32:46; Matt. 4:4

The ESV Publishing Team

The ESV publishing team has included more than a hundred people. The fourteen-member Translation Oversight Committee benefited from the work of fifty biblical experts serving as Translation Review Scholars and from the comments of the more than fifty members of the Advisory Council. This international team from many denominations shares a common commitment to the truth of God's Word and to historic Christian orthodoxy.

To God's Honor and Praise

We know that no Bible translation is perfect; but we also know that God uses imperfect and inadequate things to his honor and praise. So to God the Father, Son, and Holy Spirit—and to his people—we offer what we have done, with our prayers that it may prove useful, with gratitude for much help given, and with ongoing wonder that our God should ever have entrusted to us so momentous a task.

To God alone be the glory!
The Translation Oversight Committee

ROMANS

Greeting

1 Paul, a servant of Christ Jesus, called to be an apostle, set apart for the gospel of God, ² which he promised beforehand through his prophets in the holy Scriptures, ³ concerning his Son, who was descended from David according to the flesh ⁴ and was declared to be the Son of God in power according to the Spirit of holiness by his resurrection from the dead, Jesus Christ our Lord, ⁵ through whom we have received grace and apostleship to bring about the obedience of faith for the sake of his name among all the nations, ⁶ including you who are called to belong to Jesus Christ,

⁷ To all those in Rome who are loved by God and called to be saints:

Grace to you and peace from God our Father and the Lord Jesus Christ.

Longing to Go to Rome

⁸ First, I thank my God through Jesus Christ for all of you, because your faith is proclaimed in all the world. ⁹ For God is my witness, whom I serve with my spirit in the gospel of his Son, that without ceasing I mention you ¹⁰ always in my prayers, asking that somehow by God's will I may now at last succeed in coming to you. ¹¹ For I long to see you, that I may impart to you

some spiritual gift to strengthen you— ¹² that is, that we may be mutually encouraged by each other's faith, both yours and mine. ¹³ I do not want you to be unaware, brothers, that I have often intended to come to you (but thus far have been prevented), in order that I may reap some harvest among you as well as among the rest of the Gentiles. ¹⁴ I am under obligation both to Greeks and to barbarians, both to the wise and to the foolish. ¹⁵ So I am eager to preach the gospel to you also who are in Rome.

The Righteous Shall Live by Faith

¹⁶ For I am not ashamed of the gospel, for it is the power of God for salvation to everyone who believes, to the Jew first and also to the Greek. ¹⁷ For in it the righteousness of God is revealed from faith for faith, as it is written, "The righteous shall live by faith."

God's Wrath on Unrighteousness

¹⁸ For the wrath of God is revealed from heaven against all ungodliness and unrighteousness of men, who by their unrighteousness suppress the truth. ¹⁹ For what can be known about God is plain to them, because God has shown it to them. ²⁰ For his invisible attributes, namely, his eternal power and divine nature, have been clearly perceived, ever since the creation of the world, in the things that have been made. So they are without excuse. ²¹ For although they knew God, they did not honor him as God or give thanks to him, but they became futile in their thinking, and their foolish hearts were darkened. ²² Claiming to be wise, they became fools, ²³ and exchanged the glory of the immortal God for images resembling mortal man and birds and animals and creeping things.

I AM
not
ashamed
OF THE
gospel

ROMANS 1:16

²⁴ Therefore God gave them up in the lusts of their hearts to impurity, to the dishonoring of their bodies among themselves, ²⁵ because they exchanged the truth about God for a lie and worshiped and served the creature rather than the Creator, who is blessed forever! Amen.

²⁶ For this reason God gave them up to dishonorable passions. For their women exchanged natural relations for those that are contrary to nature; ²⁷ and the men likewise gave up natural relations with women and were consumed with passion for one another, men committing shameless acts with men and receiving in themselves the due penalty for their error.

²⁸ And since they did not see fit to acknowledge God, God gave them up to a debased mind to do what ought not to be done. ²⁹ They were filled with all manner of unrighteousness, evil, covetousness, malice. They are full of envy, murder, strife, deceit, maliciousness. They are gossips, ³⁰ slanderers, haters of God, insolent, haughty, boastful, inventors of evil, disobedient to parents, ³¹ foolish, faithless, heartless, ruthless. ³² Though they know God's righteous decree that those who practice such things deserve to die, they not only do them but give approval to those who practice them.

God's Righteous Judgment

2 Therefore you have no excuse, O man, every one of you who judges. For in passing judgment on another you condemn yourself, because you, the judge, practice the very same things. ² We know that the judgment of God rightly falls on those who practice such things. ³ Do you suppose, O man—you who judge those who practice such things and yet do them yourself—that you will escape the judgment of

God? ⁴ Or do you presume on the riches of his kindness and forbearance and patience, not knowing that God's kindness is meant to lead you to repentance? ⁵ But because of your hard and impenitent heart you are storing up wrath for yourself on the day of wrath when God's righteous judgment will be revealed.

⁶ He will render to each one according to his works: ⁷ to those who by patience in well-doing seek for glory and honor and immortality, he will give eternal life; ⁸ but for those who are self-seeking and do not obey the truth, but obey unrighteousness, there will be wrath and fury. ⁹ There will be tribulation and distress for every human being who does evil, the Jew first and also the Greek, ¹⁰ but glory and honor and peace for everyone who does good, the Jew first and also the Greek. ¹¹ For God shows no partiality.

God's Judgment and the Law

¹² For all who have sinned without the law will also perish without the law, and all who have sinned under the law will be judged by the law. ¹³ For it is not the hearers of the law who are righteous before God, but the doers of the law who will be justified. ¹⁴ For when Gentiles, who do not have the law, by nature do what the law requires, they are a law to themselves, even though they do not have the law. ¹⁵ They show that the work of the law is written on their hearts, while their conscience also bears witness, and their conflicting thoughts accuse or even excuse them ¹⁶ on that day when, according to my gospel, God judges the secrets of men by Christ Jesus.

¹⁷ But if you call yourself a Jew and rely on the law and boast in God ¹⁸ and know his will and approve what is excellent,

because you are instructed from the law; ¹⁹ and if you are sure that you yourself are a guide to the blind, a light to those who are in darkness, ²⁰ an instructor of the foolish, a teacher of children, having in the law the embodiment of knowledge and truth— ²¹ you then who teach others, do you not teach yourself? While you preach against stealing, do you steal? ²² You who say that one must not commit adultery, do you commit adultery? You who abhor idols, do you rob temples? ²³ You who boast in the law dishonor God by breaking the law. ²⁴ For, as it is written, "The name of God is blasphemed among the Gentiles because of you."

²⁵ For circumcision indeed is of value if you obey the law, but if you break the law, your circumcision becomes uncircumcision. ²⁶ So, if a man who is uncircumcised keeps the precepts of the law, will not his uncircumcision be regarded as circumcision? ²⁷ Then he who is physically uncircumcised but keeps the law will condemn you who have the written code and circumcision but break the law. ²⁸ For no one is a Jew who is merely one outwardly, nor is circumcision outward and physical. ²⁹ But a Jew is one inwardly, and circumcision is a matter of the heart, by the Spirit, not by the letter. His praise is not from man but from God.

God's Righteousness Upheld

3 Then what advantage has the Jew? Or what is the value of circumcision? ² Much in every way. To begin with, the Jews were entrusted with the oracles of God. ³ What if some were unfaithful? Does their faithlessness nullify the faithfulness of God? ⁴ By no means! Let God be true though every one were a liar, as it is written,

> "That you may be justified in your words,
>   and prevail when you are judged."

⁵ But if our unrighteousness serves to show the righteousness of God, what shall we say? That God is unrighteous to inflict wrath on us? (I speak in a human way.) ⁶ By no means! For then how could God judge the world? ⁷ But if through my lie God's truth abounds to his glory, why am I still being condemned as a sinner? ⁸ And why not do evil that good may come? — as some people slanderously charge us with saying. Their condemnation is just.

No One Is Righteous

⁹ What then? Are we Jews any better off? No, not at all. For we have already charged that all, both Jews and Greeks, are under sin, ¹⁰ as it is written:

> "None is righteous, no, not one;
> ¹¹   no one understands;
>   no one seeks for God.
> ¹²   All have turned aside; together they have become
>   worthless;
>   no one does good,
>   not even one."
> ¹³   "Their throat is an open grave;
>   they use their tongues to deceive."
>   "The venom of asps is under their lips."
> ¹⁴   "Their mouth is full of curses and bitterness."
> ¹⁵   "Their feet are swift to shed blood;
> ¹⁶   in their paths are ruin and misery,

[17]   and the way of peace they have not known."
[18]   "There is no fear of God before their eyes."

[19] Now we know that whatever the law says it speaks to those who are under the law, so that every mouth may be stopped, and the whole world may be held accountable to God. [20] For by works of the law no human being will be justified in his sight, since through the law comes knowledge of sin.

The Righteousness of God Through Faith

[21] But now the righteousness of God has been manifested apart from the law, although the Law and the Prophets bear witness to it— [22] the righteousness of God through faith in Jesus Christ for all who believe. For there is no distinction: [23] for all have sinned and fall short of the glory of God, [24] and are justified by his grace as a gift, through the redemption that is in Christ Jesus, [25] whom God put forward as a propitiation by his blood, to be received by faith. This was to show God's righteousness, because in his divine forbearance he had passed over former sins. [26] It was to show his righteousness at the present time, so that he might be just and the justifier of the one who has faith in Jesus.

[27] Then what becomes of our boasting? It is excluded. By what kind of law? By a law of works? No, but by the law of faith. [28] For we hold that one is justified by faith apart from works of the law. [29] Or is God the God of Jews only? Is he not the God of Gentiles also? Yes, of Gentiles also, [30] since God is one—who will justify the circumcised by faith and the uncircumcised through faith. [31] Do we then overthrow the

FOR ALL
HAVE

Sinned

AND FALL

Short

OF THE

Glory

OF GOD.

ROMANS 3:23

law by this faith? By no means! On the contrary, we uphold the law.

Abraham Justified by Faith

4 What then shall we say was gained by Abraham, our forefather according to the flesh? ² For if Abraham was justified by works, he has something to boast about, but not before God. ³ For what does the Scripture say? "Abraham believed God, and it was counted to him as righteousness." ⁴ Now to the one who works, his wages are not counted as a gift but as his due. ⁵ And to the one who does not work but believes in him who justifies the ungodly, his faith is counted as righteousness, ⁶ just as David also speaks of the blessing of the one to whom God counts righteousness apart from works:

7   "Blessed are those whose lawless deeds are forgiven,
          and whose sins are covered;
8   blessed is the man against whom the Lord will not
          count his sin."

⁹ Is this blessing then only for the circumcised, or also for the uncircumcised? For we say that faith was counted to Abraham as righteousness. ¹⁰ How then was it counted to him? Was it before or after he had been circumcised? It was not after, but before he was circumcised. ¹¹ He received the sign of circumcision as a seal of the righteousness that he had by faith while he was still uncircumcised. The purpose was to make him the father of all who believe without being circumcised, so that righteousness would be counted to them as well, ¹² and

to make him the father of the circumcised who are not merely circumcised but who also walk in the footsteps of the faith that our father Abraham had before he was circumcised.

The Promise Realized Through Faith

[13] For the promise to Abraham and his offspring that he would be heir of the world did not come through the law but through the righteousness of faith. [14] For if it is the adherents of the law who are to be the heirs, faith is null and the promise is void. [15] For the law brings wrath, but where there is no law there is no transgression.

[16] That is why it depends on faith, in order that the promise may rest on grace and be guaranteed to all his offspring—not only to the adherent of the law but also to the one who shares the faith of Abraham, who is the father of us all, [17] as it is written, "I have made you the father of many nations"—in the presence of the God in whom he believed, who gives life to the dead and calls into existence the things that do not exist. [18] In hope he believed against hope, that he should become the father of many nations, as he had been told, "So shall your offspring be." [19] He did not weaken in faith when he considered his own body, which was as good as dead (since he was about a hundred years old), or when he considered the barrenness of Sarah's womb. [20] No unbelief made him waver concerning the promise of God, but he grew strong in his faith as he gave glory to God, [21] fully convinced that God was able to do what he had promised. [22] That is why his faith was "counted to him as righteousness." [23] But the words "it was counted to him" were not written for his sake alone, [24] but for ours also. It will be counted to us who believe in him who raised from the dead Jesus our

Lord, [25] who was delivered up for our trespasses and raised for our justification.

Peace with God Through Faith

5 Therefore, since we have been justified by faith, we have peace with God through our Lord Jesus Christ. [2] Through him we have also obtained access by faith into this grace in which we stand, and we rejoice in hope of the glory of God. [3] Not only that, but we rejoice in our sufferings, knowing that suffering produces endurance, [4] and endurance produces character, and character produces hope, [5] and hope does not put us to shame, because God's love has been poured into our hearts through the Holy Spirit who has been given to us.

[6] For while we were still weak, at the right time Christ died for the ungodly. [7] For one will scarcely die for a righteous person—though perhaps for a good person one would dare even to die— [8] but God shows his love for us in that while we were still sinners, Christ died for us. [9] Since, therefore, we have now been justified by his blood, much more shall we be saved by him from the wrath of God. [10] For if while we were enemies we were reconciled to God by the death of his Son, much more, now that we are reconciled, shall we be saved by his life. [11] More than that, we also rejoice in God through our Lord Jesus Christ, through whom we have now received reconciliation.

Death in Adam, Life in Christ

[12] Therefore, just as sin came into the world through one man, and death through sin, and so death spread to all men because all sinned— [13] for sin indeed was in the world before

REJOICE

ROMANS 5:2

the law was given, but sin is not counted where there is no law. **14** Yet death reigned from Adam to Moses, even over those whose sinning was not like the transgression of Adam, who was a type of the one who was to come.

15 But the free gift is not like the trespass. For if many died through one man's trespass, much more have the grace of God and the free gift by the grace of that one man Jesus Christ abounded for many. **16** And the free gift is not like the result of that one man's sin. For the judgment following one trespass brought condemnation, but the free gift following many trespasses brought justification. **17** For if, because of one man's trespass, death reigned through that one man, much more will those who receive the abundance of grace and the free gift of righteousness reign in life through the one man Jesus Christ.

18 Therefore, as one trespass led to condemnation for all men, so one act of righteousness leads to justification and life for all men. **19** For as by the one man's disobedience the many were made sinners, so by the one man's obedience the many will be made righteous. **20** Now the law came in to increase the trespass, but where sin increased, grace abounded all the more, **21** so that, as sin reigned in death, grace also might reign through righteousness leading to eternal life through Jesus Christ our Lord.

Dead to Sin, Alive to God

6 What shall we say then? Are we to continue in sin that grace may abound? **2** By no means! How can we who died to sin still live in it? **3** Do you not know that all of us who have been baptized into Christ Jesus were baptized into his death? **4** We were buried therefore with him by baptism into death, in

order that, just as Christ was raised from the dead by the glory of the Father, we too might walk in newness of life.

[5] For if we have been united with him in a death like his, we shall certainly be united with him in a resurrection like his. [6] We know that our old self was crucified with him in order that the body of sin might be brought to nothing, so that we would no longer be enslaved to sin. [7] For one who has died has been set free from sin. [8] Now if we have died with Christ, we believe that we will also live with him. [9] We know that Christ, being raised from the dead, will never die again; death no longer has dominion over him. [10] For the death he died he died to sin, once for all, but the life he lives he lives to God. [11] So you also must consider yourselves dead to sin and alive to God in Christ Jesus.

[12] Let not sin therefore reign in your mortal body, to make you obey its passions. [13] Do not present your members to sin as instruments for unrighteousness, but present yourselves to God as those who have been brought from death to life, and your members to God as instruments for righteousness. [14] For sin will have no dominion over you, since you are not under law but under grace.

Slaves to Righteousness

[15] What then? Are we to sin because we are not under law but under grace? By no means! [16] Do you not know that if you present yourselves to anyone as obedient slaves, you are slaves of the one whom you obey, either of sin, which leads to death, or of obedience, which leads to righteousness? [17] But thanks be to God, that you who were once slaves of sin have become obedient from the heart to the standard of teaching to which

you were committed, ¹⁸ and, having been set free from sin, have become slaves of righteousness. ¹⁹ I am speaking in human terms, because of your natural limitations. For just as you once presented your members as slaves to impurity and to lawlessness leading to more lawlessness, so now present your members as slaves to righteousness leading to sanctification.

²⁰ For when you were slaves of sin, you were free in regard to righteousness. ²¹ But what fruit were you getting at that time from the things of which you are now ashamed? For the end of those things is death. ²² But now that you have been set free from sin and have become slaves of God, the fruit you get leads to sanctification and its end, eternal life. ²³ For the wages of sin is death, but the free gift of God is eternal life in Christ Jesus our Lord.

Released from the Law

7 Or do you not know, brothers—for I am speaking to those who know the law—that the law is binding on a person only as long as he lives? ² For a married woman is bound by law to her husband while he lives, but if her husband dies she is released from the law of marriage. ³ Accordingly, she will be called an adulteress if she lives with another man while her husband is alive. But if her husband dies, she is free from that law, and if she marries another man she is not an adulteress.

⁴ Likewise, my brothers, you also have died to the law through the body of Christ, so that you may belong to another, to him who has been raised from the dead, in order that we may bear fruit for God. ⁵ For while we were living in the flesh, our sinful passions, aroused by the law, were at work in our members to bear fruit for death. ⁶ But now we are released from the

THE

FREE

GIFT

OF GOD IS

ETERNAL

LIFE

ROMANS 6:23

law, having died to that which held us captive, so that we serve in the new way of the Spirit and not in the old way of the written code.

The Law and Sin

⁷ What then shall we say? That the law is sin? By no means! Yet if it had not been for the law, I would not have known sin. For I would not have known what it is to covet if the law had not said, "You shall not covet." ⁸ But sin, seizing an opportunity through the commandment, produced in me all kinds of covetousness. For apart from the law, sin lies dead. ⁹ I was once alive apart from the law, but when the commandment came, sin came alive and I died. ¹⁰ The very commandment that promised life proved to be death to me. ¹¹ For sin, seizing an opportunity through the commandment, deceived me and through it killed me. ¹² So the law is holy, and the commandment is holy and righteous and good.

¹³ Did that which is good, then, bring death to me? By no means! It was sin, producing death in me through what is good, in order that sin might be shown to be sin, and through the commandment might become sinful beyond measure. ¹⁴ For we know that the law is spiritual, but I am of the flesh, sold under sin. ¹⁵ For I do not understand my own actions. For I do not do what I want, but I do the very thing I hate. ¹⁶ Now if I do what I do not want, I agree with the law, that it is good. ¹⁷ So now it is no longer I who do it, but sin that dwells within me. ¹⁸ For I know that nothing good dwells in me, that is, in my flesh. For I have the desire to do what is right, but not the ability to carry it out. ¹⁹ For I do not do the good I want, but the evil I do not want is what I keep on doing. ²⁰ Now if I do what

I do not want, it is no longer I who do it, but sin that dwells within me.

²¹ So I find it to be a law that when I want to do right, evil lies close at hand. ²² For I delight in the law of God, in my inner being, ²³ but I see in my members another law waging war against the law of my mind and making me captive to the law of sin that dwells in my members. ²⁴ Wretched man that I am! Who will deliver me from this body of death? ²⁵ Thanks be to God through Jesus Christ our Lord! So then, I myself serve the law of God with my mind, but with my flesh I serve the law of sin.

Life in the Spirit

8 There is therefore now no condemnation for those who are in Christ Jesus. ² For the law of the Spirit of life has set you free in Christ Jesus from the law of sin and death. ³ For God has done what the law, weakened by the flesh, could not do. By sending his own Son in the likeness of sinful flesh and for sin, he condemned sin in the flesh, ⁴ in order that the righteous requirement of the law might be fulfilled in us, who walk not according to the flesh but according to the Spirit. ⁵ For those who live according to the flesh set their minds on the things of the flesh, but those who live according to the Spirit set their minds on the things of the Spirit. ⁶ For to set the mind on the flesh is death, but to set the mind on the Spirit is life and peace. ⁷ For the mind that is set on the flesh is hostile to God, for it does not submit to God's law; indeed, it cannot. ⁸ Those who are in the flesh cannot please God.

⁹ You, however, are not in the flesh but in the Spirit, if in fact the Spirit of God dwells in you. Anyone who does not have the Spirit of Christ does not belong to him. ¹⁰ But if Christ is in you, although the body is dead because of sin, the Spirit is life

There is
therefore
now no
Condemnation
for those
who are in
Christ Jesus

ROMANS 8:1

because of righteousness. [11] If the Spirit of him who raised Jesus from the dead dwells in you, he who raised Christ Jesus from the dead will also give life to your mortal bodies through his Spirit who dwells in you.

Heirs with Christ

[12] So then, brothers, we are debtors, not to the flesh, to live according to the flesh. [13] For if you live according to the flesh you will die, but if by the Spirit you put to death the deeds of the body, you will live. [14] For all who are led by the Spirit of God are sons of God. [15] For you did not receive the spirit of slavery to fall back into fear, but you have received the Spirit of adoption as sons, by whom we cry, "Abba! Father!" [16] The Spirit himself bears witness with our spirit that we are children of God, [17] and if children, then heirs—heirs of God and fellow heirs with Christ, provided we suffer with him in order that we may also be glorified with him.

Future Glory

[18] For I consider that the sufferings of this present time are not worth comparing with the glory that is to be revealed to us. [19] For the creation waits with eager longing for the revealing of the sons of God. [20] For the creation was subjected to futility, not willingly, but because of him who subjected it, in hope [21] that the creation itself will be set free from its bondage to corruption and obtain the freedom of the glory of the children of God. [22] For we know that the whole creation has been groaning together in the pains of childbirth until now. [23] And not only the creation, but we ourselves, who have the firstfruits of the Spirit, groan inwardly as we wait eagerly for adoption as sons, the redemption

of our bodies. [24] For in this hope we were saved. Now hope that is seen is not hope. For who hopes for what he sees? [25] But if we hope for what we do not see, we wait for it with patience.

[26] Likewise the Spirit helps us in our weakness. For we do not know what to pray for as we ought, but the Spirit himself intercedes for us with groanings too deep for words. [27] And he who searches hearts knows what is the mind of the Spirit, because the Spirit intercedes for the saints according to the will of God. [28] And we know that for those who love God all things work together for good, for those who are called according to his purpose. [29] For those whom he foreknew he also predestined to be conformed to the image of his Son, in order that he might be the firstborn among many brothers. [30] And those whom he predestined he also called, and those whom he called he also justified, and those whom he justified he also glorified.

God's Everlasting Love

[31] What then shall we say to these things? If God is for us, who can be against us? [32] He who did not spare his own Son but gave him up for us all, how will he not also with him graciously give us all things? [33] Who shall bring any charge against God's elect? It is God who justifies. [34] Who is to condemn? Christ Jesus is the one who died—more than that, who was raised—who is at the right hand of God, who indeed is interceding for us. [35] Who shall separate us from the love of Christ? Shall tribulation, or distress, or persecution, or famine, or nakedness, or danger, or sword? [36] As it is written,

"For your sake we are being killed all the day long;
    we are regarded as sheep to be slaughtered."

[37] No, in all these things we are more than conquerors through him who loved us. [38] For I am sure that neither death nor life, nor angels nor rulers, nor things present nor things to come, nor powers, [39] nor height nor depth, nor anything else in all creation, will be able to separate us from the love of God in Christ Jesus our Lord.

God's Sovereign Choice

9 I am speaking the truth in Christ—I am not lying; my conscience bears me witness in the Holy Spirit— [2] that I have great sorrow and unceasing anguish in my heart. [3] For I could wish that I myself were accursed and cut off from Christ for the sake of my brothers, my kinsmen according to the flesh. [4] They are Israelites, and to them belong the adoption, the glory, the covenants, the giving of the law, the worship, and the promises. [5] To them belong the patriarchs, and from their race, according to the flesh, is the Christ, who is God over all, blessed forever. Amen.

[6] But it is not as though the word of God has failed. For not all who are descended from Israel belong to Israel, [7] and not all are children of Abraham because they are his offspring, but "Through Isaac shall your offspring be named." [8] This means that it is not the children of the flesh who are the children of God, but the children of the promise are counted as offspring. [9] For this is what the promise said: "About this time next year I will return, and Sarah shall have a son." [10] And not only so, but also when Rebekah had conceived children by one man, our forefather Isaac, [11] though they were not yet born and had done nothing either good or bad—in order that God's purpose of election might continue, not because of works but because

of him who calls— ¹²she was told, "The older will serve the younger." ¹³As it is written, "Jacob I loved, but Esau I hated."

¹⁴What shall we say then? Is there injustice on God's part? By no means! ¹⁵For he says to Moses, "I will have mercy on whom I have mercy, and I will have compassion on whom I have compassion." ¹⁶So then it depends not on human will or exertion, but on God, who has mercy. ¹⁷For the Scripture says to Pharaoh, "For this very purpose I have raised you up, that I might show my power in you, and that my name might be proclaimed in all the earth." ¹⁸So then he has mercy on whomever he wills, and he hardens whomever he wills.

¹⁹You will say to me then, "Why does he still find fault? For who can resist his will?" ²⁰But who are you, O man, to answer back to God? Will what is molded say to its molder, "Why have you made me like this?" ²¹Has the potter no right over the clay, to make out of the same lump one vessel for honorable use and another for dishonorable use? ²²What if God, desiring to show his wrath and to make known his power, has endured with much patience vessels of wrath prepared for destruction, ²³in order to make known the riches of his glory for vessels of mercy, which he has prepared beforehand for glory— ²⁴even us whom he has called, not from the Jews only but also from the Gentiles? ²⁵As indeed he says in Hosea,

> "Those who were not my people I will call 'my people,'
>   and her who was not beloved I will call 'beloved.'"
> ²⁶ "And in the very place where it was said to them, 'You
>   are not my people,'
>   there they will be called 'sons of the living
>   God.'"

[27] And Isaiah cries out concerning Israel: "Though the number of the sons of Israel be as the sand of the sea, only a remnant of them will be saved, [28] for the Lord will carry out his sentence upon the earth fully and without delay." [29] And as Isaiah predicted,

> "If the Lord of hosts had not left us offspring,
>   we would have been like Sodom
>   and become like Gomorrah."

Israel's Unbelief

[30] What shall we say, then? That Gentiles who did not pursue righteousness have attained it, that is, a righteousness that is by faith; [31] but that Israel who pursued a law that would lead to righteousness did not succeed in reaching that law. [32] Why? Because they did not pursue it by faith, but as if it were based on works. They have stumbled over the stumbling stone, [33] as it is written,

> "Behold, I am laying in Zion a stone of stumbling,
>   and a rock of offense;
>   and whoever believes in him will not be put to
>   shame."

10 Brothers, my heart's desire and prayer to God for them is that they may be saved. [2] For I bear them witness that they have a zeal for God, but not according to knowledge. [3] For, being ignorant of the righteousness of God, and seeking to establish their own, they did not submit to God's righteousness. [4] For Christ is the end of the law for righteousness to everyone who believes.

The Message of Salvation to All

⁵ For Moses writes about the righteousness that is based on the law, that the person who does the commandments shall live by them. ⁶ But the righteousness based on faith says, "Do not say in your heart, 'Who will ascend into heaven?'" (that is, to bring Christ down) ⁷ "or 'Who will descend into the abyss?'" (that is, to bring Christ up from the dead). ⁸ But what does it say? "The word is near you, in your mouth and in your heart" (that is, the word of faith that we proclaim); ⁹ because, if you confess with your mouth that Jesus is Lord and believe in your heart that God raised him from the dead, you will be saved. ¹⁰ For with the heart one believes and is justified, and with the mouth one confesses and is saved. ¹¹ For the Scripture says, "Everyone who believes in him will not be put to shame." ¹² For there is no distinction between Jew and Greek; for the same Lord is Lord of all, bestowing his riches on all who call on him. ¹³ For "everyone who calls on the name of the Lord will be saved."

¹⁴ How then will they call on him in whom they have not believed? And how are they to believe in him of whom they have never heard? And how are they to hear without someone preaching? ¹⁵ And how are they to preach unless they are sent? As it is written, "How beautiful are the feet of those who preach the good news!" ¹⁶ But they have not all obeyed the gospel. For Isaiah says, "Lord, who has believed what he has heard from us?" ¹⁷ So faith comes from hearing, and hearing through the word of Christ.

¹⁸ But I ask, have they not heard? Indeed they have, for

"Their voice has gone out to all the earth,
     and their words to the ends of the world."

CONFESS WITH YOUR MOUTH THAT JESUS IS LORD

ROMANS 10:9

19 But I ask, did Israel not understand? First Moses says,

> "I will make you jealous of those who are not a
> nation;
> with a foolish nation I will make you angry."

20 Then Isaiah is so bold as to say,

> "I have been found by those who did not seek me;
> I have shown myself to those who did not ask for
> me."

21 But of Israel he says, "All day long I have held out my hands to a disobedient and contrary people."

The Remnant of Israel

11 I ask, then, has God rejected his people? By no means! For I myself am an Israelite, a descendant of Abraham, a member of the tribe of Benjamin. **2** God has not rejected his people whom he foreknew. Do you not know what the Scripture says of Elijah, how he appeals to God against Israel? **3** "Lord, they have killed your prophets, they have demolished your altars, and I alone am left, and they seek my life." **4** But what is God's reply to him? "I have kept for myself seven thousand men who have not bowed the knee to Baal." **5** So too at the present time there is a remnant, chosen by grace. **6** But if it is by grace, it is no longer on the basis of works; otherwise grace would no longer be grace.

7 What then? Israel failed to obtain what it was seeking. The elect obtained it, but the rest were hardened, **8** as it is written,

> "God gave them a spirit of stupor,
>   eyes that would not see
>   and ears that would not hear,
> down to this very day."

⁹ And David says,

> "Let their table become a snare and a trap,
>   a stumbling block and a retribution for them;
> 10   let their eyes be darkened so that they cannot see,
>   and bend their backs forever."

Gentiles Grafted In

¹¹ So I ask, did they stumble in order that they might fall? By no means! Rather, through their trespass salvation has come to the Gentiles, so as to make Israel jealous. ¹² Now if their trespass means riches for the world, and if their failure means riches for the Gentiles, how much more will their full inclusion mean!

¹³ Now I am speaking to you Gentiles. Inasmuch then as I am an apostle to the Gentiles, I magnify my ministry ¹⁴ in order somehow to make my fellow Jews jealous, and thus save some of them. ¹⁵ For if their rejection means the reconciliation of the world, what will their acceptance mean but life from the dead? ¹⁶ If the dough offered as firstfruits is holy, so is the whole lump, and if the root is holy, so are the branches.

¹⁷ But if some of the branches were broken off, and you, although a wild olive shoot, were grafted in among the others and now share in the nourishing root of the olive tree, ¹⁸ do not be arrogant toward the branches. If you are, remember it

is not you who support the root, but the root that supports you. [19] Then you will say, "Branches were broken off so that I might be grafted in." [20] That is true. They were broken off because of their unbelief, but you stand fast through faith. So do not become proud, but fear. [21] For if God did not spare the natural branches, neither will he spare you. [22] Note then the kindness and the severity of God: severity toward those who have fallen, but God's kindness to you, provided you continue in his kindness. Otherwise you too will be cut off. [23] And even they, if they do not continue in their unbelief, will be grafted in, for God has the power to graft them in again. [24] For if you were cut from what is by nature a wild olive tree, and grafted, contrary to nature, into a cultivated olive tree, how much more will these, the natural branches, be grafted back into their own olive tree.

The Mystery of Israel's Salvation

[25] Lest you be wise in your own sight, I do not want you to be unaware of this mystery, brothers: a partial hardening has come upon Israel, until the fullness of the Gentiles has come in. [26] And in this way all Israel will be saved, as it is written,

> "The Deliverer will come from Zion,
> he will banish ungodliness from Jacob";
> [27] "and this will be my covenant with them
> when I take away their sins."

[28] As regards the gospel, they are enemies for your sake. But as regards election, they are beloved for the sake of their forefathers. [29] For the gifts and the calling of God are irrevocable.

30 For just as you were at one time disobedient to God but now have received mercy because of their disobedience, **31** so they too have now been disobedient in order that by the mercy shown to you they also may now receive mercy. **32** For God has consigned all to disobedience, that he may have mercy on all.

33 Oh, the depth of the riches and wisdom and knowledge of God! How unsearchable are his judgments and how inscrutable his ways!

34   "For who has known the mind of the Lord,
            or who has been his counselor?"
35   "Or who has given a gift to him
            that he might be repaid?"

36 For from him and through him and to him are all things. To him be glory forever. Amen.

A Living Sacrifice

12 I appeal to you therefore, brothers, by the mercies of God, to present your bodies as a living sacrifice, holy and acceptable to God, which is your spiritual worship. **2** Do not be conformed to this world, but be transformed by the renewal of your mind, that by testing you may discern what is the will of God, what is good and acceptable and perfect.

Gifts of Grace

3 For by the grace given to me I say to everyone among you not to think of himself more highly than he ought to think, but to think with sober judgment, each according to the

measure of faith that God has assigned. [4] For as in one body we have many members, and the members do not all have the same function, [5] so we, though many, are one body in Christ, and individually members one of another. [6] Having gifts that differ according to the grace given to us, let us use them: if prophecy, in proportion to our faith; [7] if service, in our serving; the one who teaches, in his teaching; [8] the one who exhorts, in his exhortation; the one who contributes, in generosity; the one who leads, with zeal; the one who does acts of mercy, with cheerfulness.

Marks of the True Christian

[9] Let love be genuine. Abhor what is evil; hold fast to what is good. [10] Love one another with brotherly affection. Outdo one another in showing honor. [11] Do not be slothful in zeal, be fervent in spirit, serve the Lord. [12] Rejoice in hope, be patient in tribulation, be constant in prayer. [13] Contribute to the needs of the saints and seek to show hospitality.

[14] Bless those who persecute you; bless and do not curse them. [15] Rejoice with those who rejoice, weep with those who weep. [16] Live in harmony with one another. Do not be haughty, but associate with the lowly. Never be wise in your own sight. [17] Repay no one evil for evil, but give thought to do what is honorable in the sight of all. [18] If possible, so far as it depends on you, live peaceably with all. [19] Beloved, never avenge yourselves, but leave it to the wrath of God, for it is written, "Vengeance is mine, I will repay, says the Lord." [20] To the contrary, "if your enemy is hungry, feed him; if he is thirsty, give him something to drink; for by so doing you will heap burning coals on his head." [21] Do not be overcome by evil, but overcome evil with good.

LET LOVE BE GENUINE

ROMANS 12:9

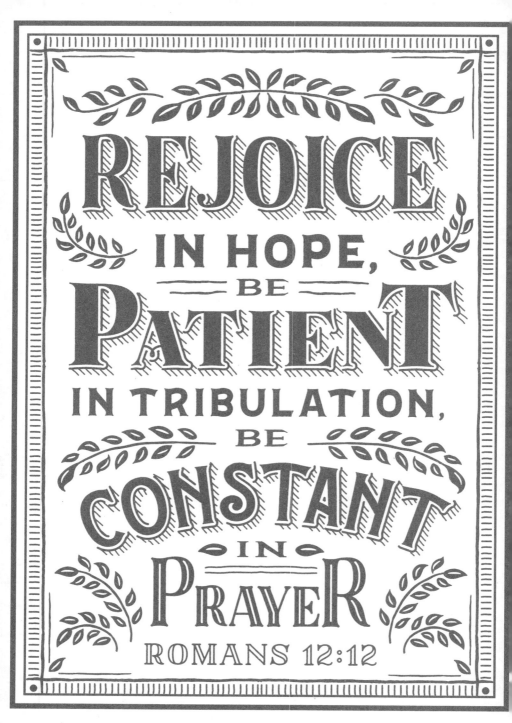

Submission to the Authorities

13 Let every person be subject to the governing authorities. For there is no authority except from God, and those that exist have been instituted by God. ² Therefore whoever resists the authorities resists what God has appointed, and those who resist will incur judgment. ³ For rulers are not a terror to good conduct, but to bad. Would you have no fear of the one who is in authority? Then do what is good, and you will receive his approval, ⁴ for he is God's servant for your good. But if you do wrong, be afraid, for he does not bear the sword in vain. For he is the servant of God, an avenger who carries out God's wrath on the wrongdoer. ⁵ Therefore one must be in subjection, not only to avoid God's wrath but also for the sake of conscience. ⁶ For because of this you also pay taxes, for the authorities are ministers of God, attending to this very thing. ⁷ Pay to all what is owed to them: taxes to whom taxes are owed, revenue to whom revenue is owed, respect to whom respect is owed, honor to whom honor is owed.

Fulfilling the Law Through Love

⁸ Owe no one anything, except to love each other, for the one who loves another has fulfilled the law. ⁹ For the commandments, "You shall not commit adultery, You shall not murder, You shall not steal, You shall not covet," and any other commandment, are summed up in this word: "You shall love your neighbor as yourself." ¹⁰ Love does no wrong to a neighbor; therefore love is the fulfilling of the law.

¹¹ Besides this you know the time, that the hour has come for you to wake from sleep. For salvation is nearer to us now

than when we first believed. [12] The night is far gone; the day is at hand. So then let us cast off the works of darkness and put on the armor of light. [13] Let us walk properly as in the daytime, not in orgies and drunkenness, not in sexual immorality and sensuality, not in quarreling and jealousy. [14] But put on the Lord Jesus Christ, and make no provision for the flesh, to gratify its desires.

Do Not Pass Judgment on One Another

14 As for the one who is weak in faith, welcome him, but not to quarrel over opinions. [2] One person believes he may eat anything, while the weak person eats only vegetables. [3] Let not the one who eats despise the one who abstains, and let not the one who abstains pass judgment on the one who eats, for God has welcomed him. [4] Who are you to pass judgment on the servant of another? It is before his own master that he stands or falls. And he will be upheld, for the Lord is able to make him stand.

[5] One person esteems one day as better than another, while another esteems all days alike. Each one should be fully convinced in his own mind. [6] The one who observes the day, observes it in honor of the Lord. The one who eats, eats in honor of the Lord, since he gives thanks to God, while the one who abstains, abstains in honor of the Lord and gives thanks to God. [7] For none of us lives to himself, and none of us dies to himself. [8] For if we live, we live to the Lord, and if we die, we die to the Lord. So then, whether we live or whether we die, we are the Lord's. [9] For to this end Christ died and lived again, that he might be Lord both of the dead and of the living.

¹⁰ Why do you pass judgment on your brother? Or you, why do you despise your brother? For we will all stand before the judgment seat of God; ¹¹ for it is written,

"As I live, says the Lord, every knee shall bow to me,
    and every tongue shall confess to God."

¹² So then each of us will give an account of himself to God.

Do Not Cause Another to Stumble

¹³ Therefore let us not pass judgment on one another any longer, but rather decide never to put a stumbling block or hindrance in the way of a brother. ¹⁴ I know and am persuaded in the Lord Jesus that nothing is unclean in itself, but it is unclean for anyone who thinks it unclean. ¹⁵ For if your brother is grieved by what you eat, you are no longer walking in love. By what you eat, do not destroy the one for whom Christ died. ¹⁶ So do not let what you regard as good be spoken of as evil. ¹⁷ For the kingdom of God is not a matter of eating and drinking but of righteousness and peace and joy in the Holy Spirit. ¹⁸ Whoever thus serves Christ is acceptable to God and approved by men. ¹⁹ So then let us pursue what makes for peace and for mutual upbuilding.

²⁰ Do not, for the sake of food, destroy the work of God. Everything is indeed clean, but it is wrong for anyone to make another stumble by what he eats. ²¹ It is good not to eat meat or drink wine or do anything that causes your brother to stumble. ²² The faith that you have, keep between yourself and God. Blessed is the one who has no reason to pass judgment on himself for what he approves. ²³ But whoever has doubts is

condemned if he eats, because the eating is not from faith. For whatever does not proceed from faith is sin.

The Example of Christ

15 We who are strong have an obligation to bear with the failings of the weak, and not to please ourselves. ² Let each of us please his neighbor for his good, to build him up. ³ For Christ did not please himself, but as it is written, "The reproaches of those who reproached you fell on me." ⁴ For whatever was written in former days was written for our instruction, that through endurance and through the encouragement of the Scriptures we might have hope. ⁵ May the God of endurance and encouragement grant you to live in such harmony with one another, in accord with Christ Jesus, ⁶ that together you may with one voice glorify the God and Father of our Lord Jesus Christ. ⁷ Therefore welcome one another as Christ has welcomed you, for the glory of God.

Christ the Hope of Jews and Gentiles

⁸ For I tell you that Christ became a servant to the circumcised to show God's truthfulness, in order to confirm the promises given to the patriarchs, ⁹ and in order that the Gentiles might glorify God for his mercy. As it is written,

> "Therefore I will praise you among the Gentiles,
>   and sing to your name."

¹⁰ And again it is said,

> "Rejoice, O Gentiles, with his people."

[11] And again,

> "Praise the Lord, all you Gentiles,
>> and let all the peoples extol him."

[12] And again Isaiah says,

> "The root of Jesse will come,
>> even he who arises to rule the Gentiles;
> in him will the Gentiles hope."

[13] May the God of hope fill you with all joy and peace in believing, so that by the power of the Holy Spirit you may abound in hope.

Paul the Minister to the Gentiles

[14] I myself am satisfied about you, my brothers, that you yourselves are full of goodness, filled with all knowledge and able to instruct one another. [15] But on some points I have written to you very boldly by way of reminder, because of the grace given me by God [16] to be a minister of Christ Jesus to the Gentiles in the priestly service of the gospel of God, so that the offering of the Gentiles may be acceptable, sanctified by the Holy Spirit. [17] In Christ Jesus, then, I have reason to be proud of my work for God. [18] For I will not venture to speak of anything except what Christ has accomplished through me to bring the Gentiles to obedience—by word and deed, [19] by the power of signs and wonders, by the power of the Spirit of God—so that from Jerusalem and all the way around to Illyricum I have fulfilled the ministry of the gospel of Christ;

²⁰ and thus I make it my ambition to preach the gospel, not where Christ has already been named, lest I build on someone else's foundation, ²¹ but as it is written,

> "Those who have never been told of him will see,
> and those who have never heard will
> understand."

Paul's Plan to Visit Rome

²² This is the reason why I have so often been hindered from coming to you. ²³ But now, since I no longer have any room for work in these regions, and since I have longed for many years to come to you, ²⁴ I hope to see you in passing as I go to Spain, and to be helped on my journey there by you, once I have enjoyed your company for a while. ²⁵ At present, however, I am going to Jerusalem bringing aid to the saints. ²⁶ For Macedonia and Achaia have been pleased to make some contribution for the poor among the saints at Jerusalem. ²⁷ For they were pleased to do it, and indeed they owe it to them. For if the Gentiles have come to share in their spiritual blessings, they ought also to be of service to them in material blessings. ²⁸ When therefore I have completed this and have delivered to them what has been collected, I will leave for Spain by way of you. ²⁹ I know that when I come to you I will come in the fullness of the blessing of Christ.

³⁰ I appeal to you, brothers, by our Lord Jesus Christ and by the love of the Spirit, to strive together with me in your prayers to God on my behalf, ³¹ that I may be delivered from the unbelievers in Judea, and that my service for Jerusalem may be acceptable to the saints, ³² so that by God's will I may come to

you with joy and be refreshed in your company. ³³ May the God of peace be with you all. Amen.

Personal Greetings

16 I commend to you our sister Phoebe, a servant of the church at Cenchreae, ² that you may welcome her in the Lord in a way worthy of the saints, and help her in whatever she may need from you, for she has been a patron of many and of myself as well.

³ Greet Prisca and Aquila, my fellow workers in Christ Jesus, ⁴ who risked their necks for my life, to whom not only I give thanks but all the churches of the Gentiles give thanks as well. ⁵ Greet also the church in their house. Greet my beloved Epaenetus, who was the first convert to Christ in Asia. ⁶ Greet Mary, who has worked hard for you. ⁷ Greet Andronicus and Junia, my kinsmen and my fellow prisoners. They are well known to the apostles, and they were in Christ before me. ⁸ Greet Ampliatus, my beloved in the Lord. ⁹ Greet Urbanus, our fellow worker in Christ, and my beloved Stachys. ¹⁰ Greet Apelles, who is approved in Christ. Greet those who belong to the family of Aristobulus. ¹¹ Greet my kinsman Herodion. Greet those in the Lord who belong to the family of Narcissus. ¹² Greet those workers in the Lord, Tryphaena and Tryphosa. Greet the beloved Persis, who has worked hard in the Lord. ¹³ Greet Rufus, chosen in the Lord; also his mother, who has been a mother to me as well. ¹⁴ Greet Asyncritus, Phlegon, Hermes, Patrobas, Hermas, and the brothers who are with them. ¹⁵ Greet Philologus, Julia, Nereus and his sister, and Olympas, and all the saints who are with them. ¹⁶ Greet one another with a holy kiss. All the churches of Christ greet you.

Final Instructions and Greetings

[17] I appeal to you, brothers, to watch out for those who cause divisions and create obstacles contrary to the doctrine that you have been taught; avoid them. [18] For such persons do not serve our Lord Christ, but their own appetites, and by smooth talk and flattery they deceive the hearts of the naive. [19] For your obedience is known to all, so that I rejoice over you, but I want you to be wise as to what is good and innocent as to what is evil. [20] The God of peace will soon crush Satan under your feet. The grace of our Lord Jesus Christ be with you.

[21] Timothy, my fellow worker, greets you; so do Lucius and Jason and Sosipater, my kinsmen.

[22] I Tertius, who wrote this letter, greet you in the Lord.

[23] Gaius, who is host to me and to the whole church, greets you. Erastus, the city treasurer, and our brother Quartus, greet you.

Doxology

[25] Now to him who is able to strengthen you according to my gospel and the preaching of Jesus Christ, according to the revelation of the mystery that was kept secret for long ages [26] but has now been disclosed and through the prophetic writings has been made known to all nations, according to the command of the eternal God, to bring about the obedience of faith— [27] to the only wise God be glory forevermore through Jesus Christ! Amen.